I Was Early in the World

Kevin Ryan

Published by New Generation Publishing in 2024

Copyright © Kevin Ryan 2024

First Edition

ISBN: 978-1-83563-350-2

www.newgeneration-publishing.com

New Generation Publishing

QUEEN OF HEARTS

You thought you sought fun,

Lawned and housed hill

Sped like an elf down,

Scruffy boys chase,

Who swoon soon will in the

Tempest your gaze made.

How easy they all their

Pride risk for you,

Follow so love – struck like

Devotees do;

Pearls whirl,

They wet the air,

Slink in the shower those boys.

My left – behind heart

So glad for you was.

Each of them craves your arm circle him may,

So you both where boughs shade

On the grassy hill lay.

OTHER ME

By the wave I

Doctor your eyes,

You a different

Man see,

Baying gulls that plague a bay

Bayed above the other me.

Sprays your face freeze,

Scamps below the cold gold disc

Moody elder wrath risk;

Whole days pass, no

Words your mouth leave,

Bears down long a

Low grey fleece,

Sullen those crows streak,

Birds on air that's

Black whirr,

Move and dive and

Stars breed.

I clay shell of a world crack,

Into your sleep seep.

WHEN HE YOUR NAME SAYS

Far are the lights that a necklace make,

So the sprawl rim'll glimmer,

Sleep the scamp tame.

Night his limbs still.

They on their backs after play pant,

Turf under crush.

You wonder how deep touch your heart I may

When home trail the others.

To mist turned your whisper,

Frail frame on grass lain.

Pain is a blade to my heart when you leave.

Under black river the cargo rolled slow on,

Lost you are on suburban lawn,

Cold when kids call in growing dark,

Beyond your gate lark.

When he your name says to see if you hear,
If it ring on the air,
See if you his nearness miss,
Bid him come again, no light but starlight,
And shoeless in your room walk.

WE TRAINS

If the globe is circular,

Why do trains

Run flat?

Do they chortle to hurtle,

Startle

Circled – earth believers

Dead in their tracks?

Wham them flat on their backs with the facts that,

However round you

Prove earth to be,

We, with unfettered glee,

On terrain flat as pancakes

Run free,

Flatter than you on your back under

Wagons on the track.

If a doughnut - shaped globe in the

Hollows of space spins,

It only remains to assert more than ever,

We trains run flat,

Flat as you on your back,

Flat as the flat black track

We run over.

SIMON FINDS THE MENU

Simon sought the menu

Wishing to know what the Pain Of The Day was,

Found the menu under the table and it said,

Pain Of The Day: nothing specific,

Just a general, overall pain that you

Can't really pinpoint,

Simon thought, That's terrific,

Non – pinpointed pain is

Pain Of The Day,

Caring not what other diners chose

He ordered straightaway,

Let them eat cake for all it matters to me, he thought

And ordered Pain Of The Day.

A little later the

Busy street beckoned,

He wasted not a second in

Rushing outside,

Wore his pain with pride,

No one at his side to

Comfort as he moved in the

Cloudy world he roved.

But Simon reached the edge of night

And there the pain of the day

Was by his dark and dreamless sleep

Gently soothed away.

IN A WAY, THIN GIRL

In a way, thin girl,

Where waves at

Mossy brick slop,

Where who wish, when it's dark, you would

A little love swap,

Studded with diamonds like

Starry eyes have they draped sable heaven,

And you slender – framed gift are,

As deep in your coat

Curled fingers sink.

It's too cold where you walk that

Hand – me – downs you stole warm,

They want your gaunt limbs near,

Flint heart melted.

Run to girlish fun you would,

Worlds beyond a grim tide's lap,

Where sleep is rare,

Bone below your eye pale,

Frail the soul tramps

Fell into love with.

Arm – flailingly and

Head – first,

Steeply and

Deeply into cold

Love fell.

They tried to

Please through

Freezing streets

And you

Wouldn't turn round,

Sound of your scorn

Burned a

Wound on his heart.

In a way, thin girl,

You sate my yearn,

Please my eye,

Moving on a lane

Stir pain in my breast,

Cause the crest – fallen follow where

Vapours from river rise.

HUNGRY CHILDREN

We're at a gutter scruffy,

Kerb – close wheels still,

Along the jam a

Whine of trapped men.

The sun was making the city wilt,

I guilt – plagued knelt

To my plea send.

It was summer and barefoot girls

Go slowly by,

Summer now and town slowed down

Still as sky was.

We climbed to a room haunt,

Floorboard lords whose

Grimy rags flap.

It was summer to the ends of avenues,

Breeze billowed her hair

Where a child ran,

Her foot on the slab rang.

Your voice sang,

From the bedless floor where I lay rose.

O, it's deep the alone-ness,

In the chill see the mob move,

To where they into love fall,

Its wiles like a dove – call

In the mouth of a girl coo.

But *you* city at night roam,

Foams to your bridge glide.

Hide us, wily children call,

Grant us a roof for the skies pound.

They solemn trudge and,

Weary on the stairway,

High as your unlocked door go.

DECEIVERS TALK SWEET

So many leaves through the autumn pile

That I can't make sense of the voices anymore,

I daily woke to a riddle on the rise

 And at a doorway mooch.

The frown was dark of he who came before me,

On echoing cobbles in grimy lanes,

His speech was hard, his brow of iron,

I dodge like a cat to step out of his chains,

I at a sea – edge gaze,

Exit plan from a distant maze,

Dawdling duos pass.

A woman's fingers once traced my frame,

But such was my fame she only saw with one eye,

That high in a panic on the roof of a train

I rode by in the night that she trusted for sleep.

They play the piped music, the scandal they bleat,

I hear not a note,

Nor a word that they say,

The villains don't fool me,

Whose tongue is sweet,

I skulk in the towns where they

Whisper like a church.

I warmed to a girl but she

Cradled me coldly,

With patchwork heart,

Veil of fake beauty,

Wounded me mutely on a soft bed at night,

So I warned her with frowns down a

Dark freezing street.

WHEN THEY TRAIN BELOW THE MOON BOARD

They down the waves wade,

Flail, thresh,

Flesh through its pores sea – soaked,

They delete their crimes would,

As foams their feet drown.

Noon rails glisten,

He shouldering guilt stoops,

Riders his face scan,

Suns upon his anguish burn,

They a deadline chase,

Pace a platform,

Uneasy on fate wait.

They delve a riddle of hurt,

Stars rise and hawks wheel,

He'll hear the words they hurl to wound,

When they train below the moon board.

Passers – by who slowly pass

Really hurtle do,

Their worst curse on rogues heap,

Before the sleep they inherit forever.

Rogues who in a metropolis lost

Did peeling rooms haunt,

Gauntly cold behold the dusk,

No soul hear speak,

Sneak to a niche that they

Shiver in peace may,

Outstay villains skilled to taunt and,

Where their limbs lay,

Say, we'll see no rest,

Long as these bones at

Behest of heaven stray.

WHEN I HAD GOLD

When light is leaving and

Giants across the fields stride,

When I by you ride,

Slow roads a maze make,

I to nowhere be wish,

But you by me sit,

Lawns in the glass pass,

I feign you're a bride

And our ride bumps.

This side of town

The nameless,

Blameless,

No loud garb flaunt;

None of them know me,

Behind my bones get,

Take me to their heart,

I outlaw am on a high – rise lawn.

Called my name a voice at night,
On mud and frost I
Slim child hug,

Hugged her forever, though when
Twilit chill grew
She twist out of view would.

When I had gold
By me in a room,
Crimson as sky was her
Breath on my neck.

We head – bowed ran
For rain on the drama spat,

Silver in our hair,
Till beads on the air cease.

STILL PAD SHACKLED

O you still

Pad shackled,

Cloud brood over,

Driftwood – like

Cold at the walls move.

Lit city walk,

Murk the bank laps,

Slug – slow waters tap.

Swift click the locks where you

Mustn't belong.

Wrongly veer so the

Quick law swoops,

Swaying footfall they say

Takes you crimeward.

When I yet lived,

I'd wake to the ache the

Rise of the morn brought,

The riddle and fear,

If only instead they'd me in sleep keep.

How they howl as dawn lifts,

O keep me in sleep do.

Spare a tired shoe that

Hike of long hunger.

CLAIM YOU THERE

I my way up to

Air claw,

Have lone on that

Street limped,

Gaunt at

Gutter sagged.

Wish kiss for comfort

Stained lips would.

I used to your

Fingers touch,

Hold them as holy,

Lowly for your welcome that,

Though you others love,

I fell into glad.

Sad was summer,

Drops black smack and the roads gleam,

Dream you if you didn't show I would,

Claim you there with my

Rare heart pulsing.

RATTLE

They won't find a hollower

Rattle than mine if they

Stab and quiz,

Say the bedless,

Soothed by

Juice who

Loose a lament to waves.

Daylight slaughtered my sleep, said one,

What will keep this wolf at bay?

I see them say as they

Trippers on the pier hear,

Sea a girder column whipping,

Solemn did they fakely vow,

Weary me and wear me down,

All I said worthless under their feet,

They handsomer souls than me

Speed to greet,

And this rattle spurn.

Gold seas move,

Black turn,

Heave they did when the

Moon struck,

Streets I step so still lay,

That ache unsaid throbs,

They even in sleep weep.

Sad vista rain stung,

I alone slabs slap,

Walls loom and the skies clap,

I hollow in a frayed jacket rattle,

They prattle and bet on an outcome of weather,

Nothing of this

Yearn learn.

Desolate vista rain stung,

We hungry hid when she swarmed,

Under lock and key my voice kept,

You should have wept that I

Chained in the fray stay.

Girls who perch on the pier

Peer seaward,

Seaweed to

Unshoed feet clung,

How low was their sun hung,

They don't know who I am,

And light is going on the

Shore they drift from.

OVER

He won't give you anymore
Poetry,
It would joyless jar now,

To your ear like a
Curse come,

As rainy scorn on your
Roof the skies spit.

I sang you in my mouth till today,
Prayed in vain, let her
Changeless stay.

But they don't heed prayers,
They only let
Hunger in my bones strain.

They let unsunned day cloud;

Where neat lawns gleam I've seen the

Ghost who your face wears.

,

CANAL

Nightly, at
Still canals,
Damn history the
Guilt – laden.

Fogs drift,

They fist clench,

Crave a bed as the street sleeps.

Cats by wavelet lap creep.

Kill our crime, the guilty weep.

All our wrongs hide
At the side of canals,
Where we in the cold move.

I SPAT SPARKS

I spat sparks for
Wrong jealousy,
Wouldn't look straight,
Her heart hurt;

Look right, look
Left,
Deftly bird sky skims,
Your hurt heart under.

I'm a fool who
Spat sparks,

Not a single joy lingers
Where fingers in sand traced.

STOLE THIS FREEDOM

Freedom of bleak school that,

Childless,

Streaked are its hollow halls,

Lights from a street glare;

And stagger, stagger,

Drunk with tears,

Crying down the lonely years,

To its portals,

To its halls,

Moonlit walls

No inmate shield

When stars hang.

I steal this freedom,

Roads wet without,

No footfall ring with.

Later they fill with bustle shall,

I cold on tiles lay,

Can't know what these bones mean,

Moon streams clear at dark a.m. ,

Edges of sky sob.

I shed the other freedom,

Vast as a world it was and I

That freedom shed in shadow

Till sun rays rise and buds shine.

Preen the strutters,

Day blooms and I

Solemn where they grin watch.

Cars charge to roads fill,

Chilly kids run,

Nightly did the moon stun,

Tiles I roamed when

Dead till dawn the town was.

Sly plotters crime plan,

I stand in the freedom the

Dark that steals your voice gave.

And the rays reach,

Gold on my bones they

Each to the wall gleam.

THOSE AT WAR FALL

While those at

War fall,

That awful lust must all

Their prey track,

Yet lovers, where sun

Spill will,

On a gilded shore sway.

Battle -zone smoke

Choke lovers of war will,

Who hunt the harmless,

They woes pile on the

Souls who sleep lose.

WE DONE WITH SLUMBER MERGE

Did you remember me,

Blazered where the crowd be,

How small I was,

Cloistered yard and mist rose.

Misfits done with slumber merge,

Through bleak halls surge to

Rigid and mute be.

Much as they can their wound lick,

Fingers clean and woes moan.

Reign high over mud

Deaf gods they curse.

YOU CAN COME TO ME

You can come to me tonight,
Around the time of the fading light,
You can come to me very soon,
I kept the things you gave me,
I'll be here for you maybe,
You can come to me out of the gloom.

And if the day leaves you defeated,
And though you try you are mistreated,
Till the dusk that finds you all alone
Closes round your worrying head,
Come and see about me instead,
In the mysterious, flickering twilight zone.

And maybe, when we've closed the door,
You'll hear words you never heard before,
And maybe for yourself I'll save

A little love I never gave before.

Not long since we met,I can even remember it yet,

Not long since I saw you there,

Looking like nobody gave you

Nothing that could ever save you,

Like a ride to somewhere far from here.

The day leaves you defeated,

Though you try you're still mistreated

And the dusk that finds you all alone

Closes round your worrying head,

Come and see about me instead

In the mysterious, flickering twilight zone.

WILL YOU MY SAINTHOOD SING

Will you maybe my sainthood sing,

Lyricless song,

One as wrong as me hasn't lived,

Trod the long maze.

Desolate beach lashed,

Mournful sky hung,

Sung call of gull gone,

Who atop wave rode

When I used to your hand hold.

Will you surely my falsehood say,

So I fold in shame may,

Till sad train halts that

Bear me away will.

YOU IN THE SPANISH ROOM SAT

Ice – blue peaks of mount rays pierce,

I tiny at their base walked,

Vast their oldness,

Cold my whole skin so I

Snow – thin blink where

Sink in sky do

High tips of rock;

Split the lips that under them plead.

In the warm room

You're the one my

Fingers feel;

Below our feet

Souls in street through

Town rush and trial rue.

Vessels in the moon move,
Children in the sun run;

After savage mountain
You in the wings wait,
To cross my path come.

NEAR NOVEMBER

Frost froze your lane,

You frail and the cold clung,

Had you in this hand

Chilly - fingered hand slipped

The griefs I cup would

Count for nothing;

Not if eyes the

Freeze made water

Look when I bend

To your mouth meet;

Sleet tapped the pane,

Light left;

Soft as I can

Down the dim hall

I move to the milk-white
Bones claim.

ryan wrote in london when he was small. later he
wrote in spain for a while. he is the author of the
following volumes:

OVER JUNE LANE

DARKLY UNDER SUN

KEYHOLDER

STRAY LIKE YOU

BECK OF TIDE

EVE WAS SCARLET

his songs "One Day" and "The Way They Look At
You" appear on YouTube.

9 781835 633502